To:

From:

D0341146

Born to Shop®

Without Stress My Life Would Be Empty

PETER PAUPER PRESS, INC.
White Plains, New York

Born to Shop®

Copyright © 2008 Paper Island Limited.
All rights reserved.

Book designed by Heather Zschock

Published by Peter Pauper Press, Inc.
202 Mamaroneck Avenue
White Plains, NY 10601
All rights reserved
ISBN 978-1-59359-818-1
Printed in China

7 6 5 4 3 2 1

Visit us at www.peterpauper.com

Contents

Introduction 5

Got Stress? 6

Coping 39

Introduction

All stressed out and no chocolate in sight? We've all been there, girlfriend, muddling through the endless workweek, underpaid, underappreciated, and overburdened . . . when the realization hits that this is not the life we ordered. And with that thought comes the freedom to indulge in the joys of procrastination and self-indulgence. After all, "stressed" is only "desserts" spelled backwards!

Take coping to a whole new level as you multitask with some serious attitude, major retail therapy, a freezer full of ice cream, a little bit of blissful ignorance, and the freedom to emerge from your own little world now and then just long enough to smell the coffee. Stress may come in all sizes, but it's nothing that can't be managed with a little feisty wit, a wedge of lime, and a shot of tequila.

Got Stress?

If you look like your passport photo, you're not well enough to travel.

Today's agenda... get through it!

Never put off until **tomorrow** what you can **avoid** doing **altogether.**

On the keyboard of life always keep one finger on the escape button.

It's been
Monday
all week.

Domestically challenged

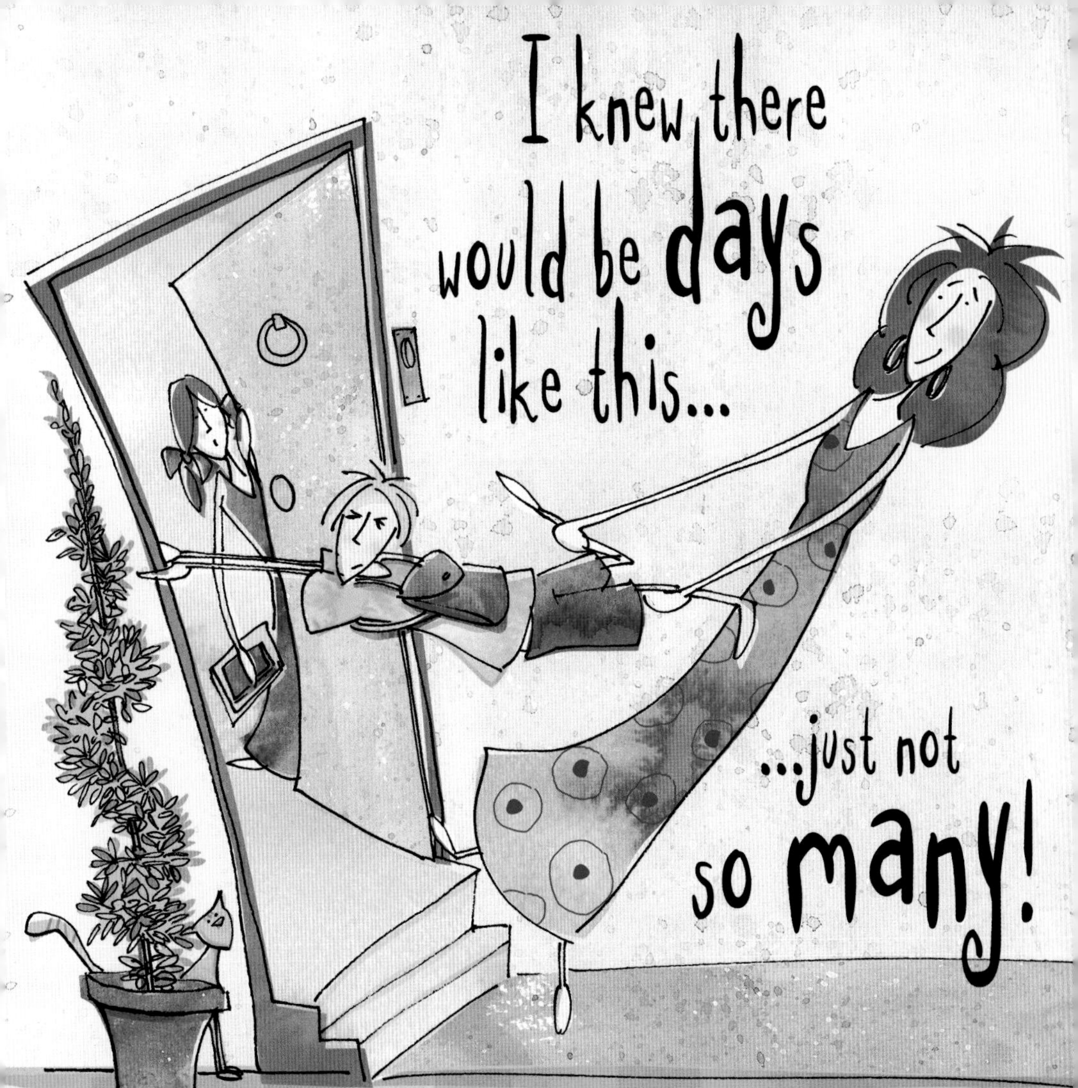
I knew there would be days like this...
...just not so many!

Alcohol doesn't cause hangovers, waking up does.

I would be
unstoppable
if I could
just get
started.

You can't control everything, your hair was put on your head to remind you of that.

Gray hair is **hereditary,** we get it from our **children.**

I earn a six figure salary— pity about the decimal point!

Cheer up! Retirement's only 30 years away.

I understand the concepts of cooking and cleaning
just not how they apply to me.
S
P

Home wasn't built in a day.

I love mornings, I just wish they came later in the day.

I always wanted to be **somebody**, but now I realize I should have been **more specific.**

Coping

With age comes wisdom... big deal.

I may be
late
but
I'm worth
the
wait.

do not rush

23

I'm in my
own world,
it's ok,
they know me
here.

I take life with a
pinch of salt, a wedge
of lime, and a shot
of tequila.

Kids get colds, men get flu, women get on with it.

Hard work pays off in the future, laziness pays off now.

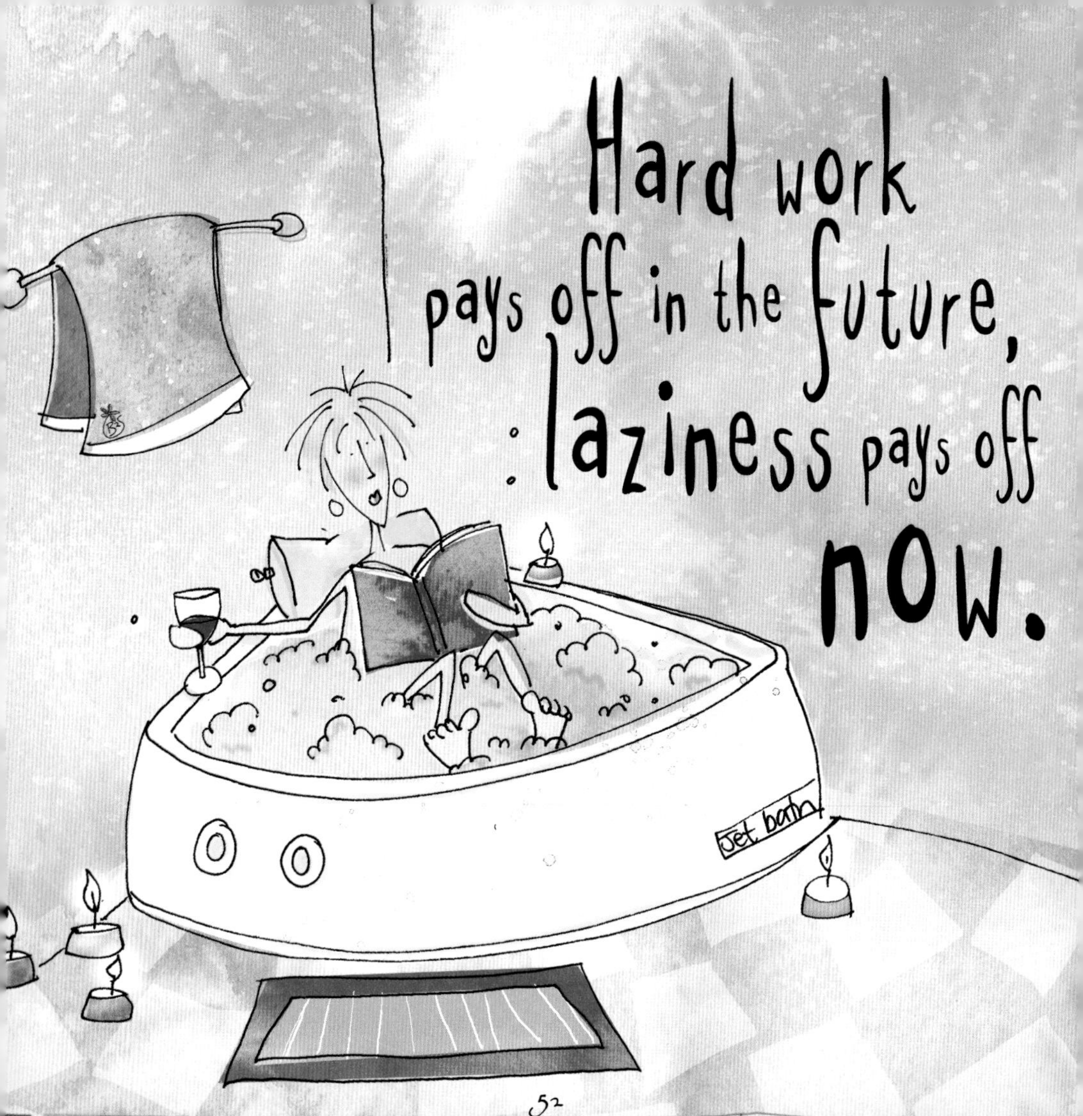

I know I'm not perfect, but I'm so close it scares me.

Lead me **not** into temptation, I can find the way **myself**.

I never met
a calorie I
didn't
like.

If the shoe
fits buy it
in every
color.

We may not have it all together...

...but together we have it all.

The best
man for
the job
is a
woman.

I always give 100% at work... 15% Monday, 20% Tuesday, 40% Wednesday, 20% Thursday and 5% Friday.

When you **don't know** what you're **doing** walk **fast** and **look worried.**

63

Tough cookies
don't
crumble.

Instead of cleaning the house, I just turn the lights out.

I'm only as strong as the coffee I drink and the hairspray I use.

All the coffee in Colombia won't make me a morning person.

Behind every
successful
woman is a
cat and a
fridge full of
chocolate.